100 Hot Licks for
PEDAL STEEL GUITAR
ESSENTIAL SOLOING PHRASES FOR E9 TUNING

BY

Johnie Helms

T0081832

PLAYBACK+
Speed • Pitch • Balance • Loop

To access audio, visit:
www.halleonard.com/mylibrary

7337-9625-2016-2119

Cover Photo: Tim Whims

ISBN 978-1-4584-9729-1

HAL•LEONARD®

Copyright © 2013 by HAL LEONARD CORPORATION
International Copyright Secured   All Rights Reserved

No part of this publication may be reproduced in any form or by
any means without the prior written permission of the Publisher.

Visit Hal Leonard Online at
www.halleonard.com

Contact us:
Hal Leonard
7777 West Bluemound Road
Milwaukee, WI 53213
Email: info@halleonard.com

In Europe, contact:
Hal Leonard Europe Limited
42 Wigmore Street
Marylebone, London, W1U 2RN
Email: info@halleonardeurope.com

In Australia, contact:
Hal Leonard Australia Pty. Ltd.
4 Lentara Court
Cheltenham, Victoria, 3192 Australia
Email: info@halleonard.com.au

CONTENTS

INTRODUCTION

Welcome to *100 Hot Licks for Pedal Steel Guitar*. These licks are arranged for E9 tuning and range in difficulty from extremely easy to more advanced. Although each lick has been played in a certain key, bear in mind that virtually all of them may be played in any key you choose. Just move your bar to the proper position to transpose the lick. Once you learn a lick, however, don't stop there. Try combining them to make longer phrases or complete solos. After all, that's what most solos are—a continuous combination of many smaller licks and phrases.

Note: On the accompanying recording, you may hear what's referred to as "cabinet noise," which is a normal characteristic of the instrument.

PEDAL SETUP

		Pedals				Knee Levers		
		A	B	C	D	E	F	G
F#	1							G
D#	2					D		
G#	3		A					
E	4			F#	D#		F	
B	5	C#		C#				
G#	6		A					
F#	7							G
E	8				D#		F	
D	9					C#		
B	10	C#						

4

 ## LICK #1: Key of E

TRACK 1

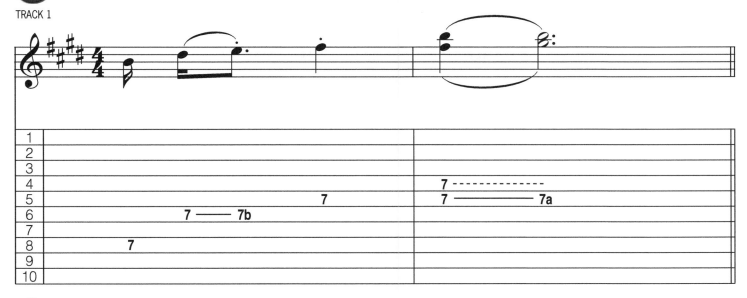

LICK #2: Key of E

TRACK 1
cont'd

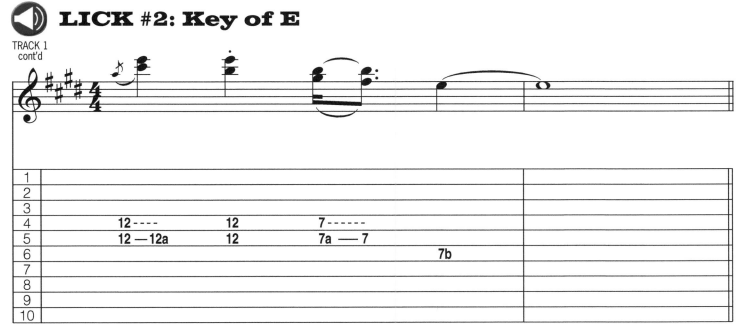

LICK #3: Key of E

TRACK 2

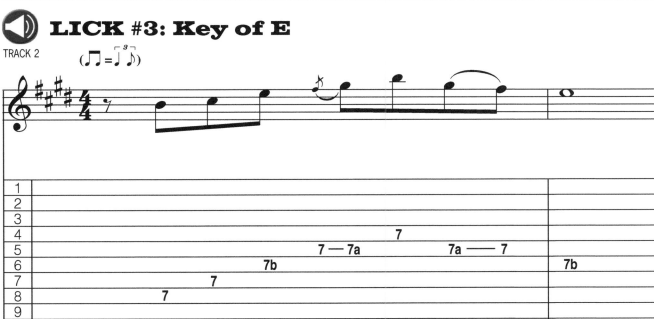

LICK #4: Key of E

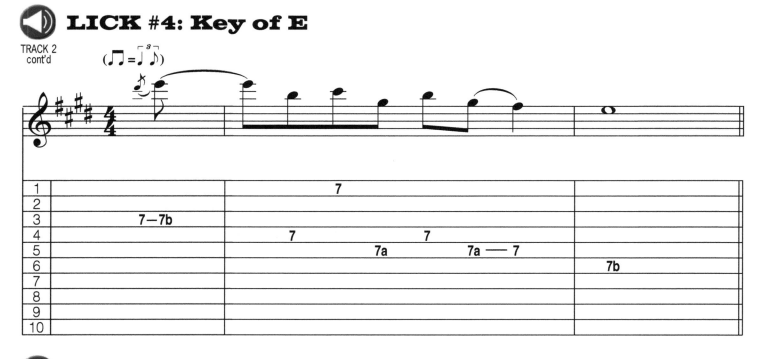

LICK #5: Key of E

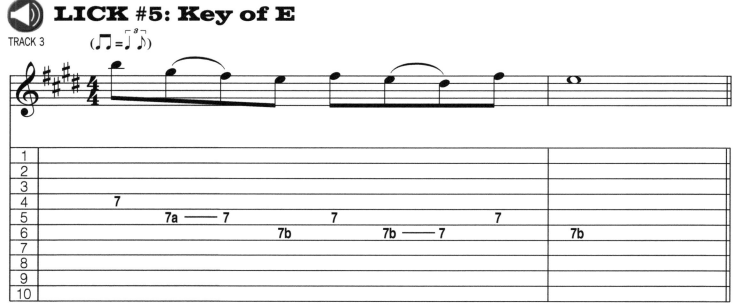

LICK #6: Key of C

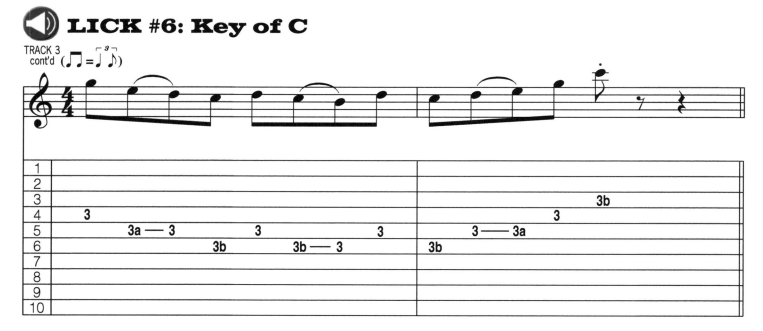

LICK #7: Key of C

TRACK 4

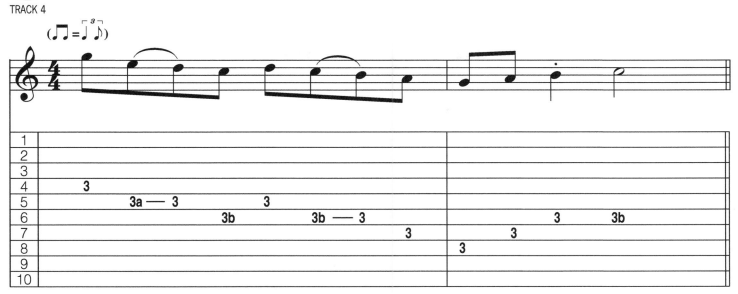

LICK #8: Key of C

TRACK 4
cont'd

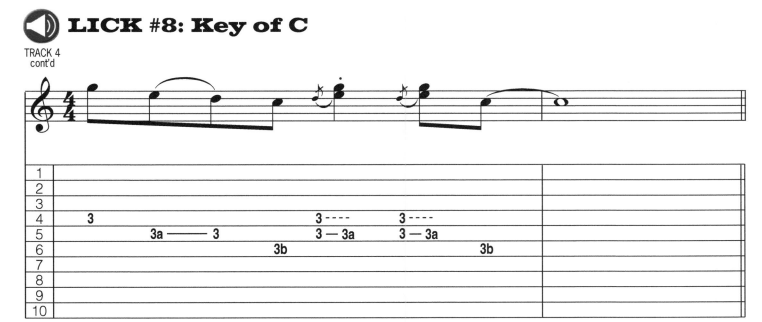

LICK #9: Key of C

TRACK 5

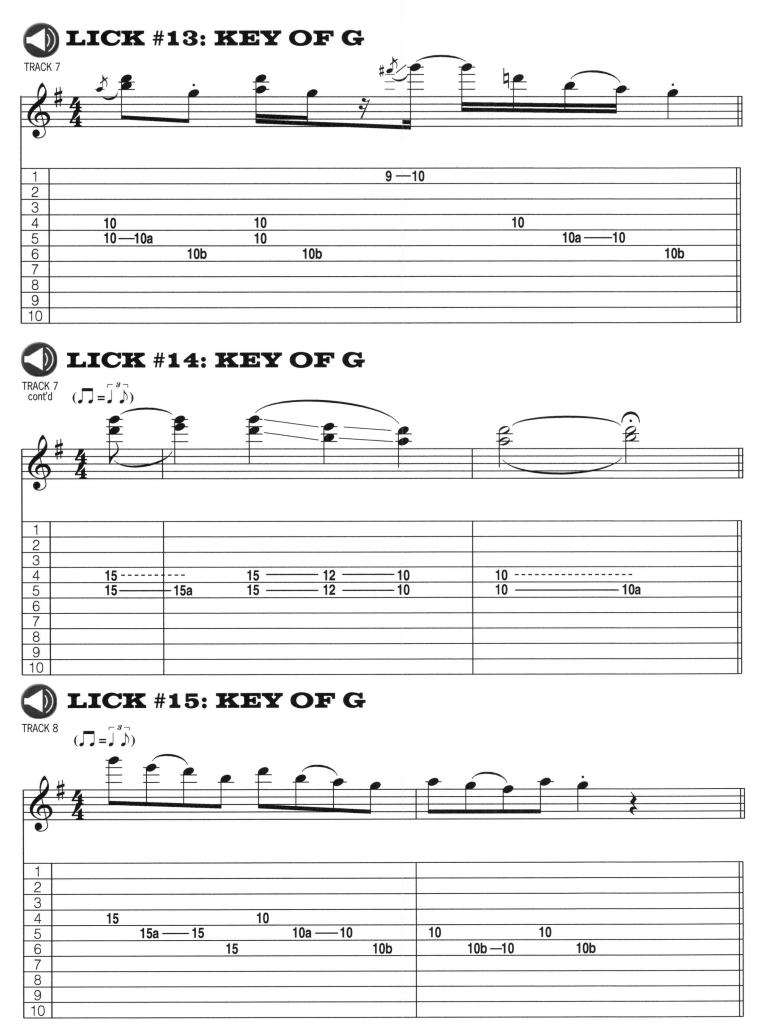

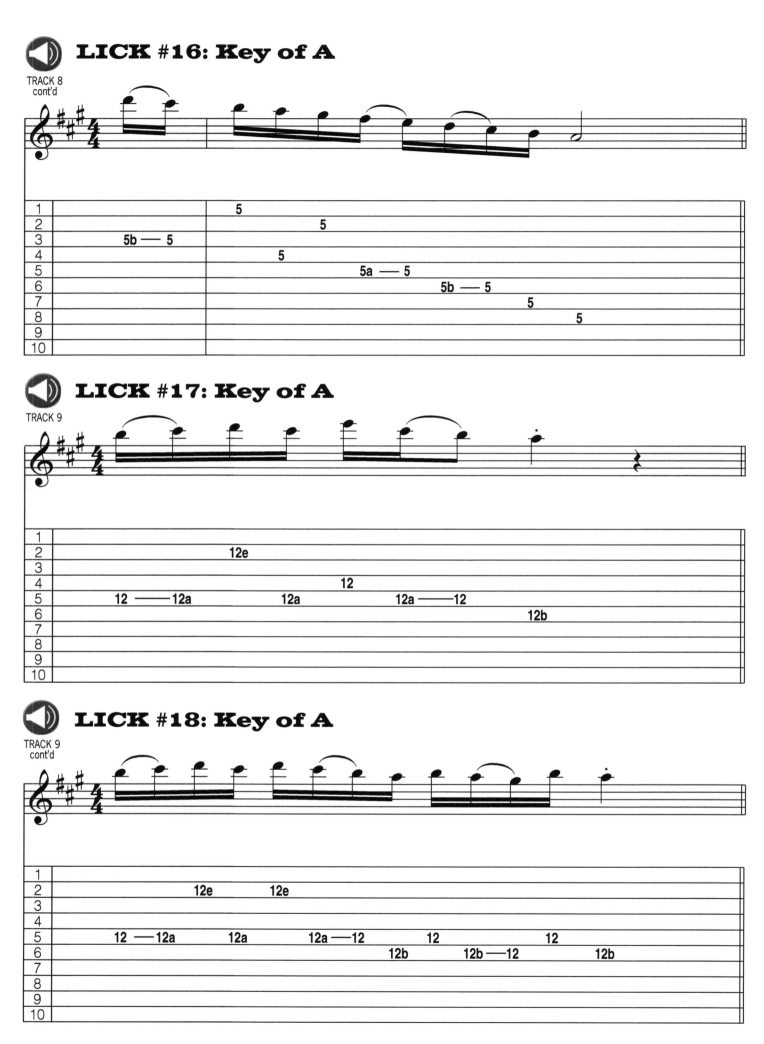

LICK #19: Key of A

TRACK 10

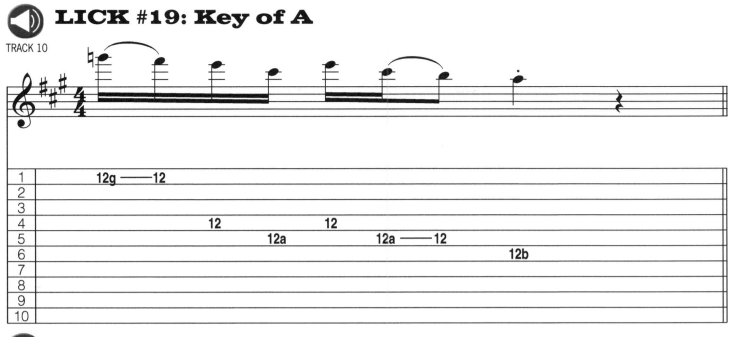

LICK #20: Key of A

TRACK 10
cont'd

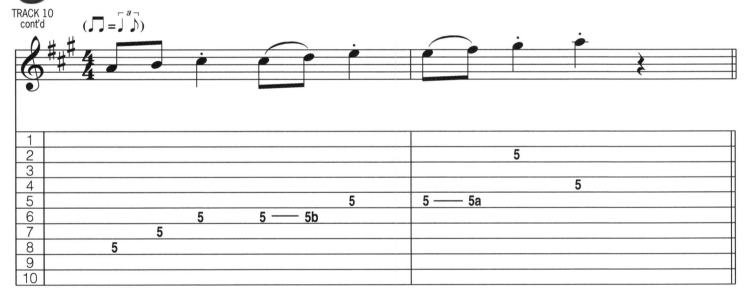

LICK #21: Key of D

TRACK 11

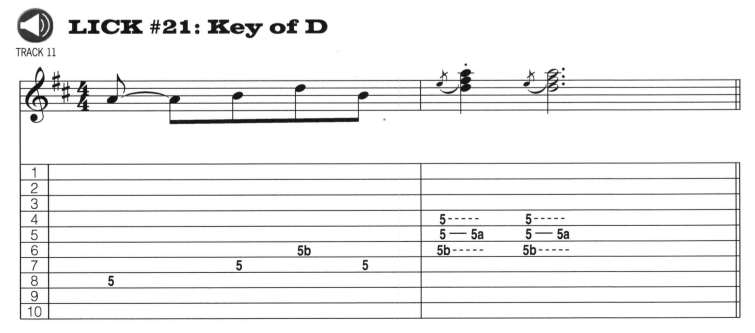

LICK #22: Key of D

TRACK 11
cont'd

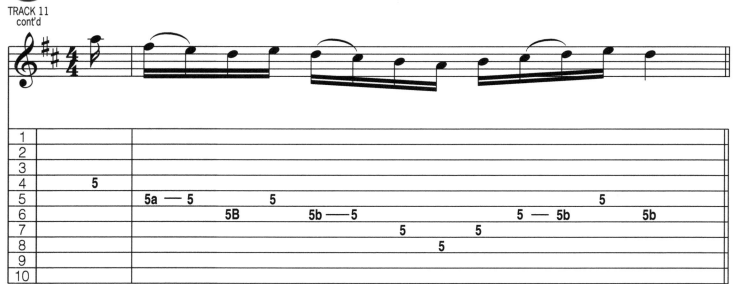

1											
2											
3											
4	5										
5		5a — 5		5						5	
6			5B		5b —5				5 — 5b		5b
7						5		5			
8							5				
9											
10											

LICK #23: Key of D

TRACK 12

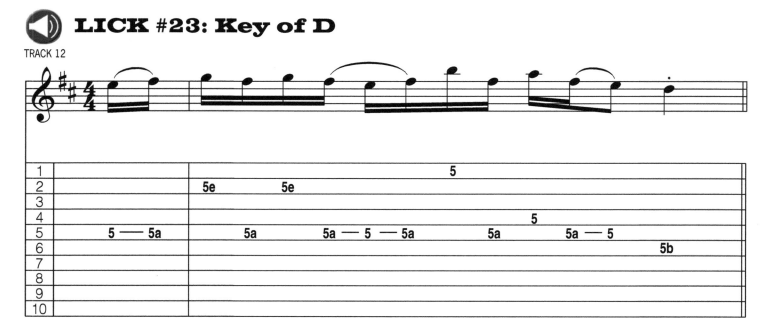

1						5				
2			5e	5e						
3										
4							5			
5		5 — 5a	5a	5a — 5 — 5a		5a	5a — 5		
6									5b
7									
8									
9									
10									

LICK #24: Key of D

TRACK 12
cont'd

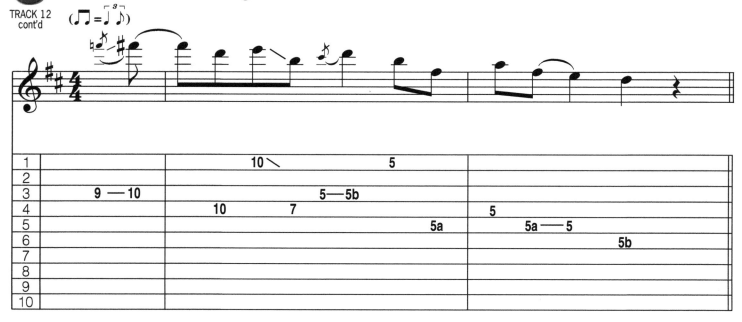

1			10↘		5		
2							
3		9 — 10			5—5b		
4			10	7		5	
5					5a	5a — 5	
6							5b
7							
8							
9							
10							

LICK #25: Key of D

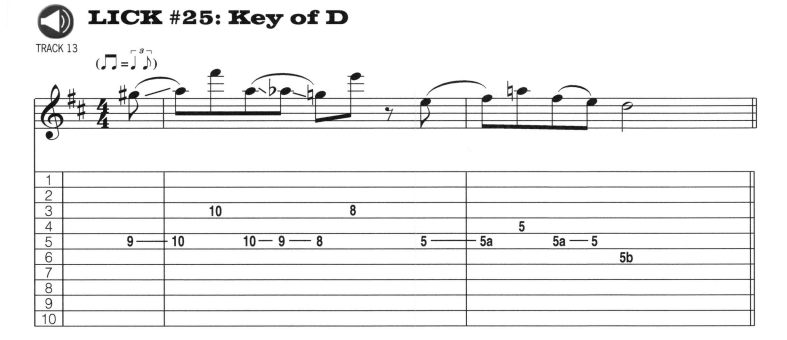

LICK #26: Key of C

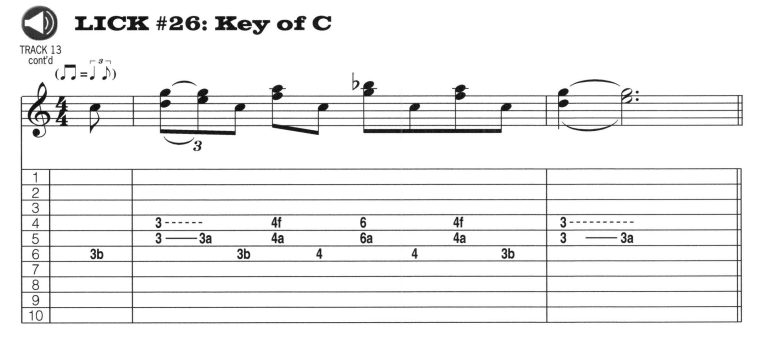

LICK #27: Key of C

LICK #28: Key of C

TRACK 14
cont'd

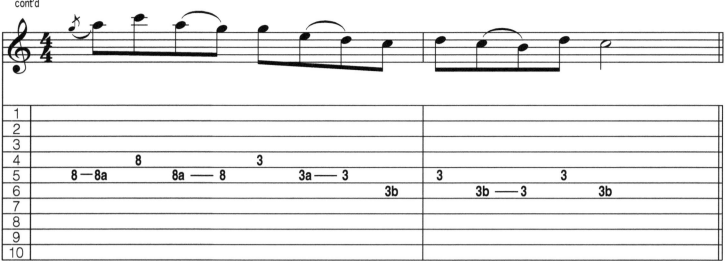

1		
2		
3		
4	8 3	
5	8 — 8a 8a — 8 3a — 3	3 3
6	3b	3b — 3 3b
7		
8		
9		
10		

LICK #29: Key of C

TRACK 15

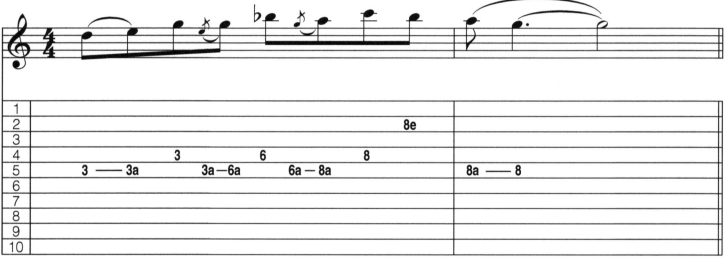

1		
2	8e	
3		
4	3 6 8	
5	3 — 3a 3a — 6a 6a — 8a	8a — 8
6		
7		
8		
9		
10		

LICK #30: Key of C

TRACK 15
cont'd

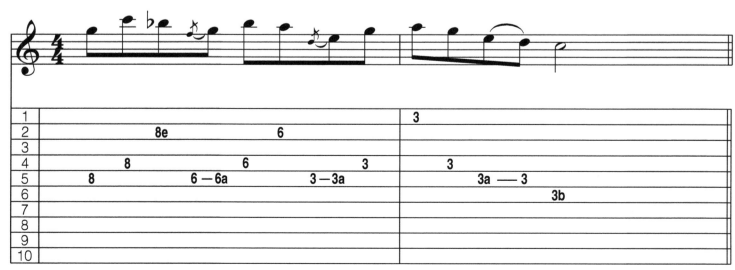

1		3
2	8e 6	
3		
4	8 6 3	3
5	8 6 — 6a 3 — 3a	3a — 3
6		3b
7		
8		
9		
10		

LICK #31: Key of F

TRACK 16

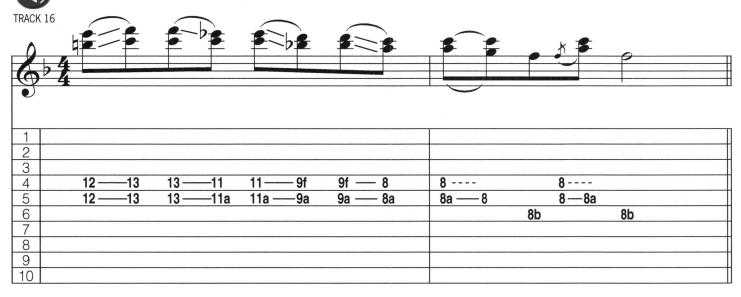

String													
1													
2													
3													
4	12 — 13	13 — 11	11 — 9f	9f — 8		8 - - - -		8 - - - -	
5	12 — 13	13 — 11a	11a — 9a	9a — 8a		8a — 8		8 — 8a	
6							8b		8b
7									
8									
9									
10									

LICK #32: Key of F

TRACK 16
cont'd

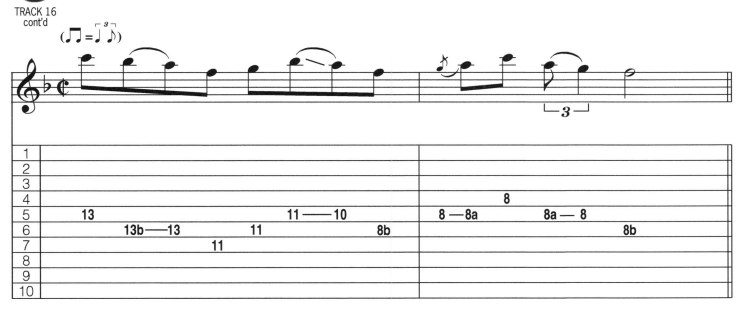

String								
1								
2								
3								
4					8			
5	13		11 — 10	8 — 8a	8a — 8			
6		13b — 13	11	8b			8b	
7		11						
8								
9								
10								

LICK #33: Key of F

TRACK 17

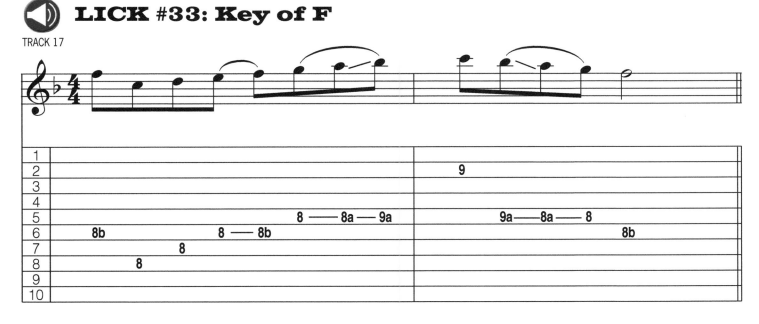

String							
1							
2				9			
3							
4							
5		8 — 8a — 9a	9a — 8a — 8				
6	8b	8 — 8b			8b		
7	8						
8	8						
9							
10							

LICK #34: Key of F

TRACK 17
cont'd

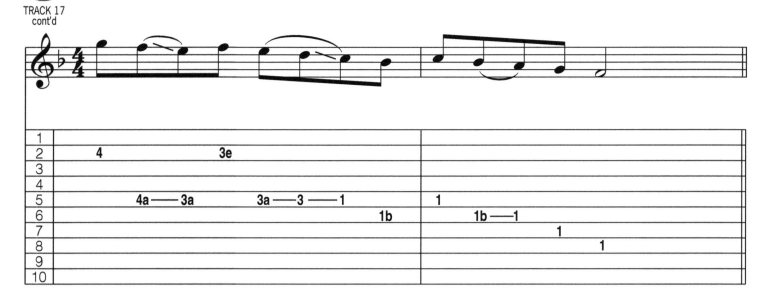

1						
2	4		3e			
3						
4						
5	4a — 3a		3a — 3 — 1		1	
6				1b	1b — 1	
7						1
8						1
9						
10						

LICK #35: Key of F

TRACK 18

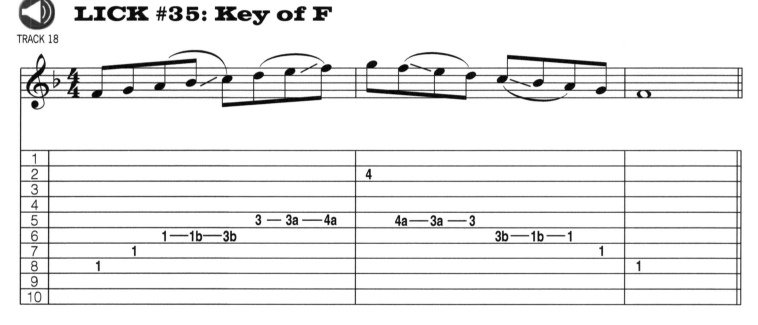

1					
2			4		
3					
4					
5		3 — 3a — 4a	4a — 3a — 3		
6	1 — 1b — 3b			3b — 1b — 1	
7	1			1	
8	1				1
9					
10					

LICK #36: Key of B

TRACK 18
cont'd

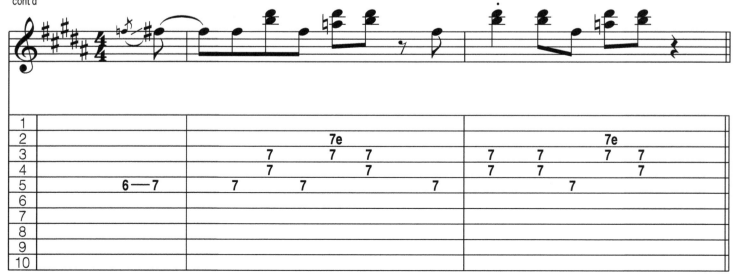

1											
2				7e					7e		
3			7	7	7		7	7		7	7
4			7		7		7	7			7
5	6 — 7	7	7			7		7			
6											
7											
8											
9											
10											

LICK #37: Key of B

TRACK 19

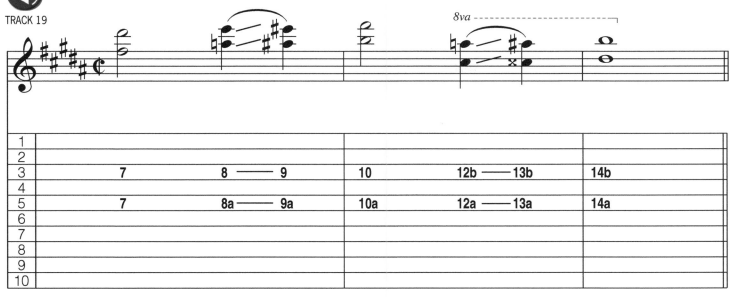

1						
2						
3	7	8 — 9	10	12b — 13b	14b	
4						
5	7	8a — 9a	10a	12a — 13a	14a	
6						
7						
8						
9						
10						

LICK #38: Key of B

TRACK 19
cont'd

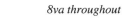

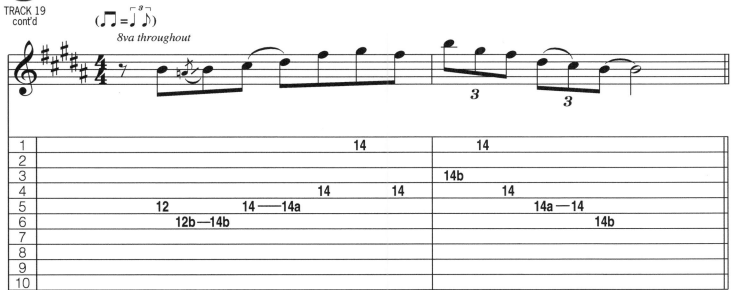

1			14	14	
2					
3				14b	
4		14	14	14	
5	12	14 —14a		14a —14	
6	12b—14b				14b
7					
8					
9					
10					

LICK #39: Key of B

TRACK 20

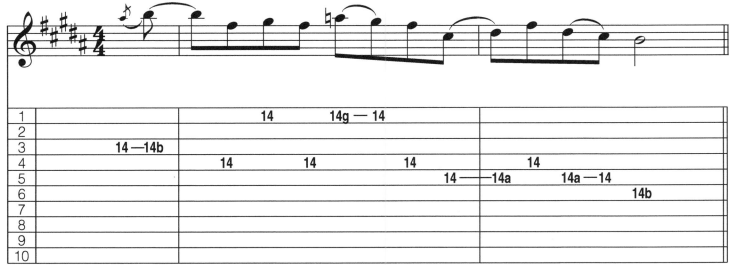

1		14	14g — 14		
2					
3	14 —14b				
4		14	14	14	14
5				14 —14a	14a —14
6					14b
7					
8					
9					
10					

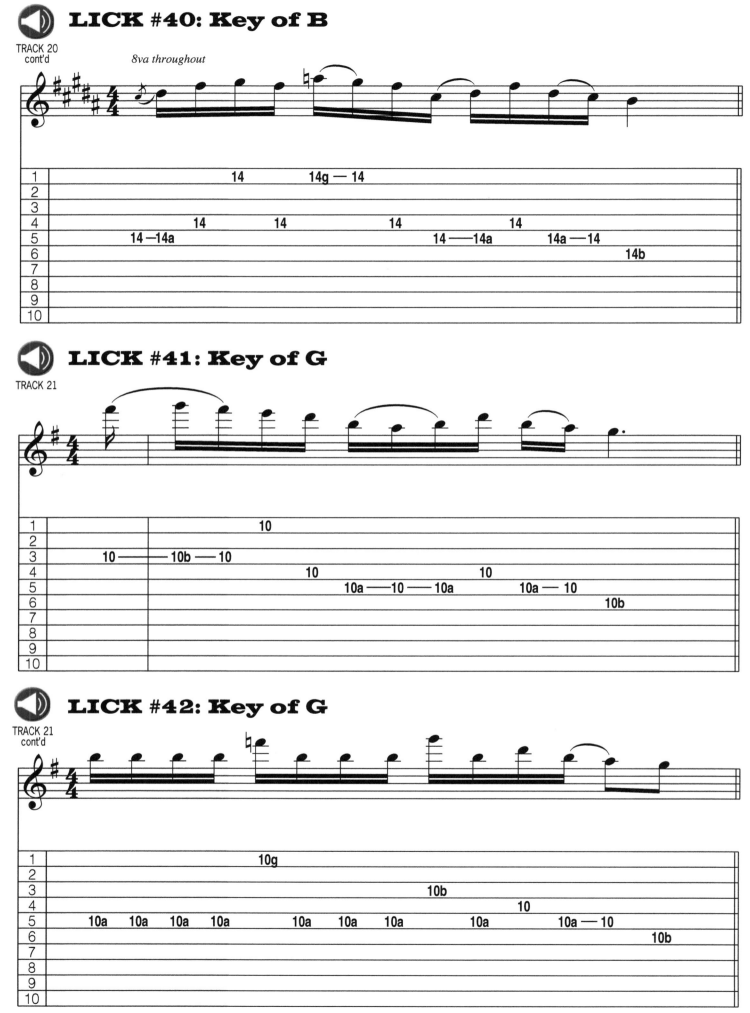

LICK #43: Key of G

TRACK 22

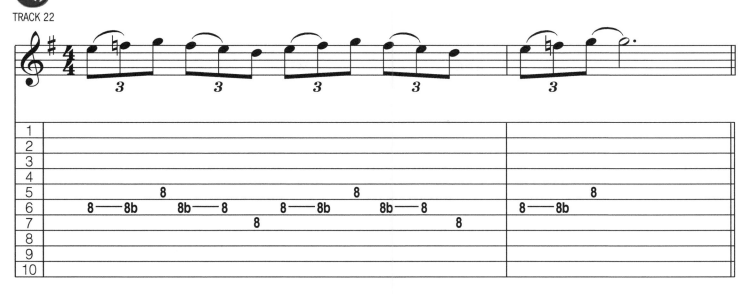

1			
2			
3			
4			
5	8	8	8
6	8—8b 8b—8	8—8b 8b—8	8—8b
7	8	8	
8			
9			
10			

LICK #44: Key of G

TRACK 22
cont'd

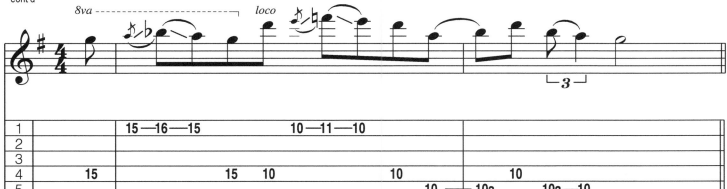

1	15—16—15	10—11—10	
2			
3			
4	15	15 10 10	10
5		10—10a	10a—10
6			10b
7			
8			
9			
10			

LICK #45: Key of G

TRACK 23

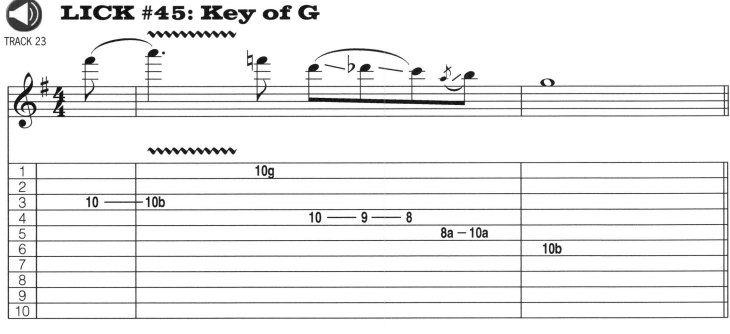

1		10g	
2			
3	10—10b		
4		10—9—8	
5		8a—10a	
6			10b
7			
8			
9			
10			

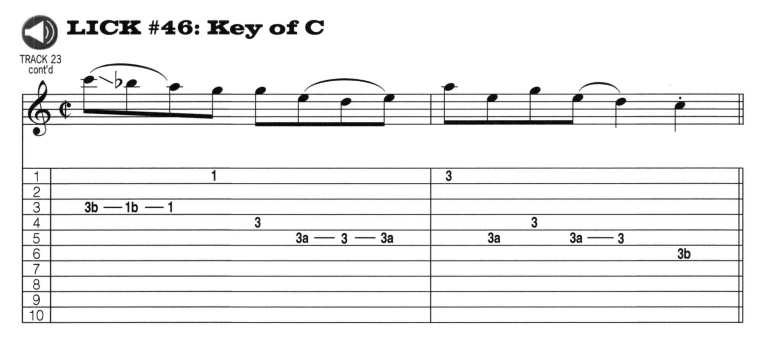

LICK #46: Key of C

1		1	3
2			
3	3b — 1b — 1		
4		3	3
5		3a — 3 — 3a	3a 3a — 3
6			3b
7			
8			
9			
10			

LICK #47: Key of C

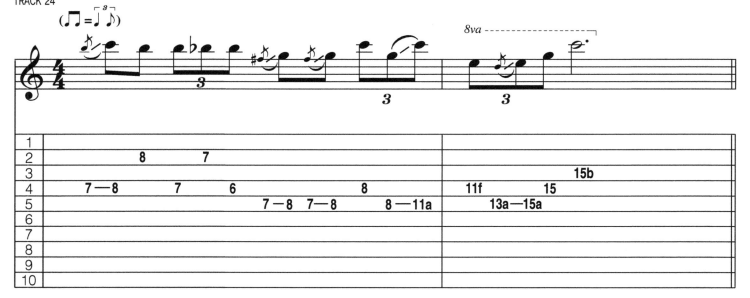

1			
2	8 7		
3			15b
4	7 — 8 7 6	8	11f 15
5		7 — 8 7 — 8 8 — 11a	13a—15a
6			
7			
8			
9			
10			

LICK #48: Key of C

8va throughout

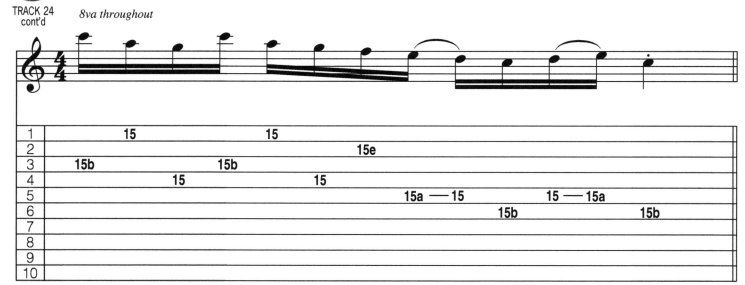

1	15	15	
2		15e	
3	15b	15b	
4	15	15	
5		15a — 15	15 — 15a
6		15b	15b
7			
8			
9			
10			

LICK #49: Key of C

TRACK 25

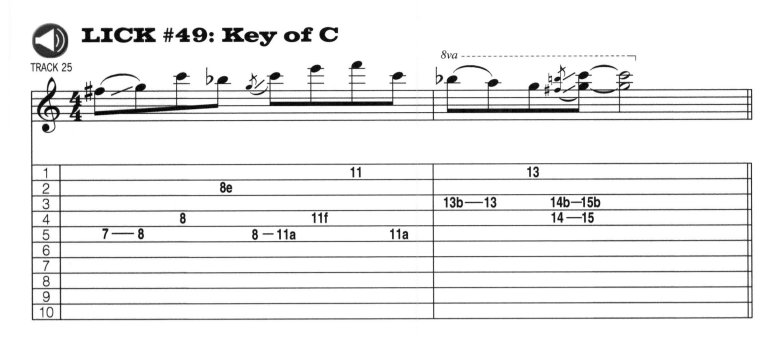

LICK #50: Key of C

TRACK 25
cont'd

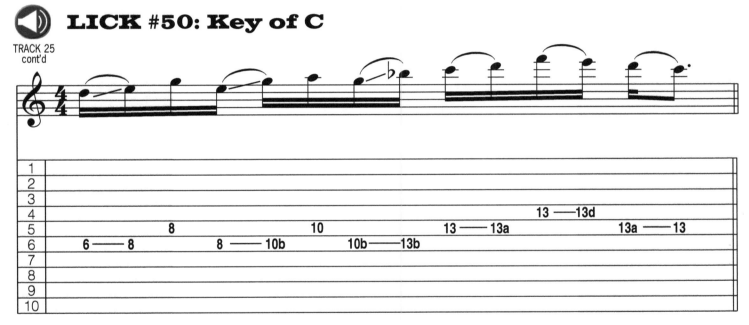

LICK #51: Key of E

TRACK 26

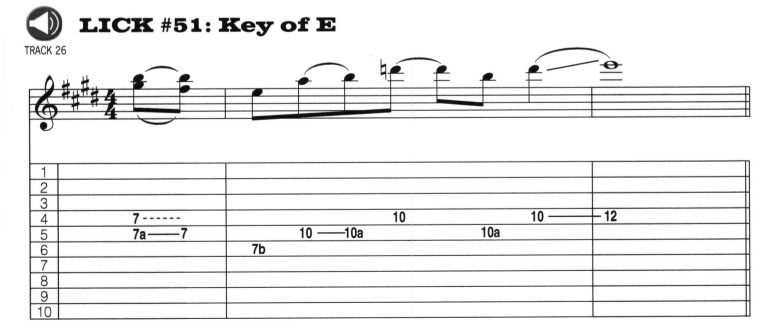

LICK #52: Key of E

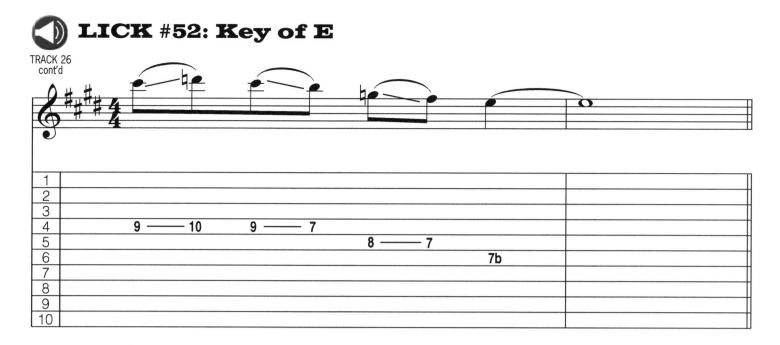

LICK #53: Key of E

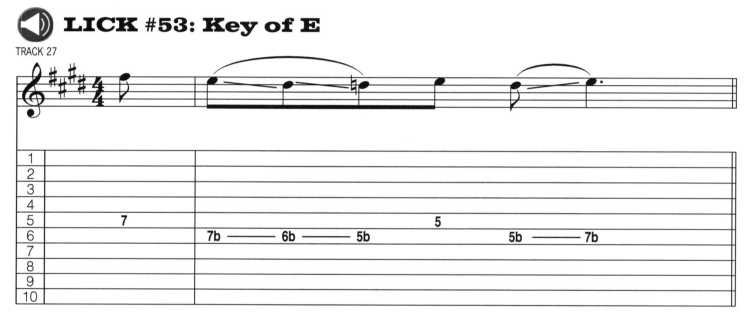

LICK #54: Key of E

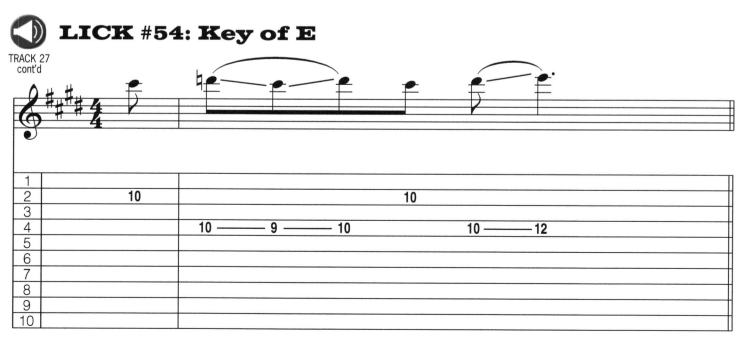

LICK #55: Key of E

TRACK 28

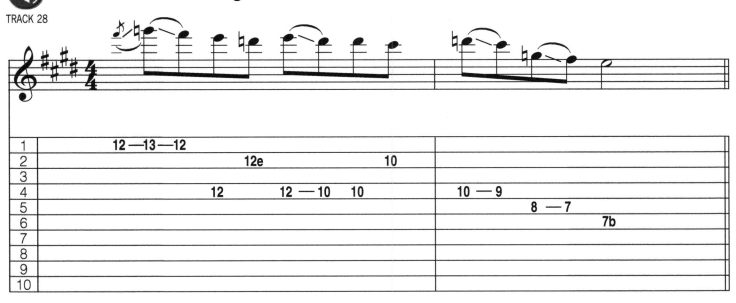

LICK #56: Key of A

TRACK 28
cont'd

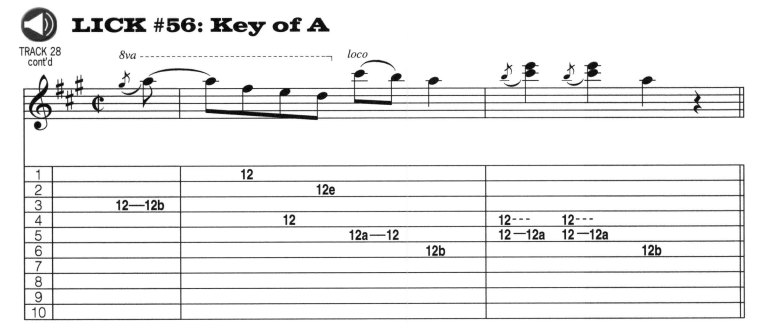

LICK #57: Key of A

TRACK 29

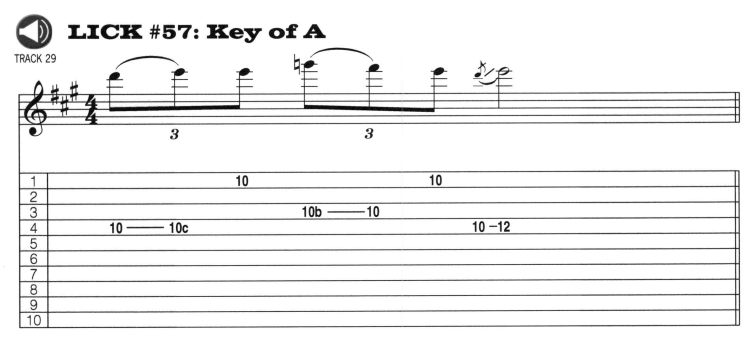

LICK #58: Key of Em

TRACK 29
cont'd

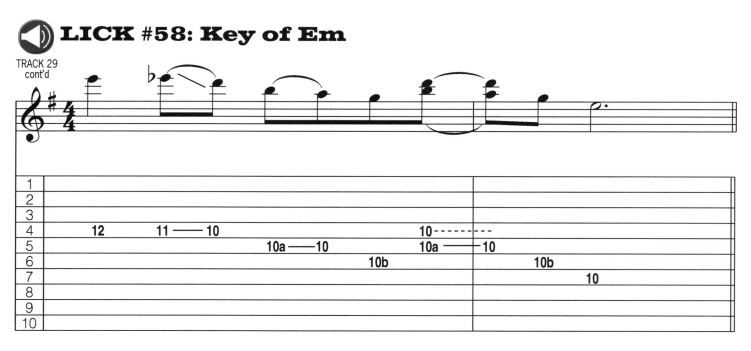

1			
2			
3			
4	12 11 —— 10		10---------
5	10a —10	10a —10	
6	10b	10b	
7		10	
8			
9			
10			

LICK #59: Key of Em

TRACK 30

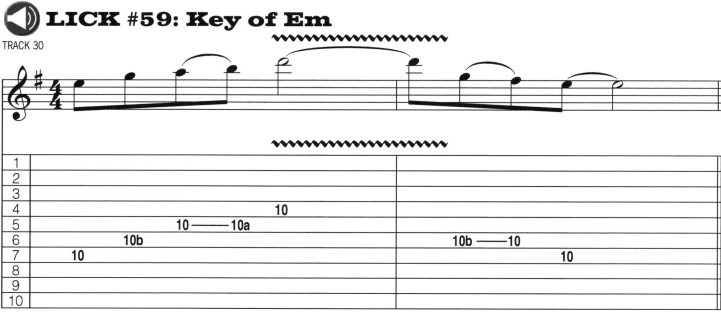

1			
2			
3			
4	10		
5	10 —— 10a		
6	10b	10b —10	
7	10	10	
8			
9			
10			

LICK #60: Key of A

TRACK 30
cont'd

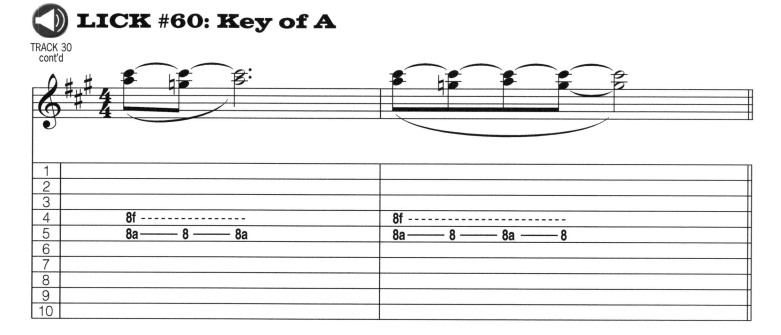

1			
2			
3			
4	8f ----------------	8f -------------------------	
5	8a—— 8 —— 8a	8a—— 8 —— 8a —— 8	
6			
7			
8			
9			
10			

LICK #61: Key of F

TRACK 31

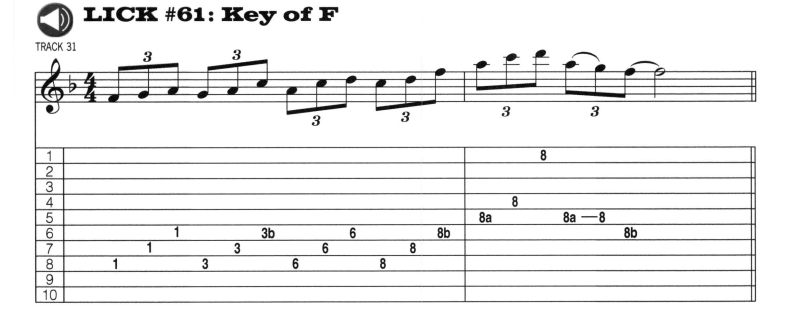

LICK #62: Key of F

TRACK 31
cont'd

LICK #63: Key of F

TRACK 32

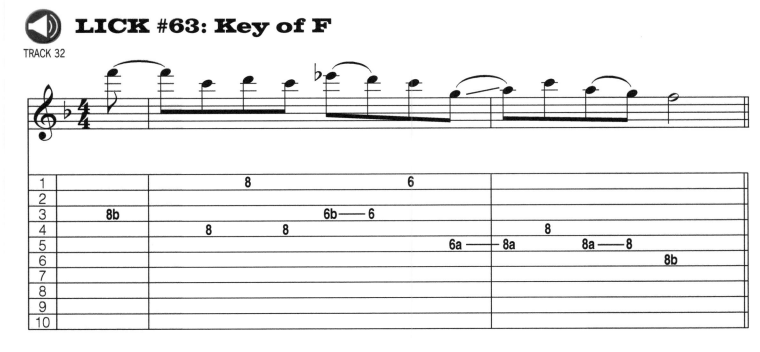

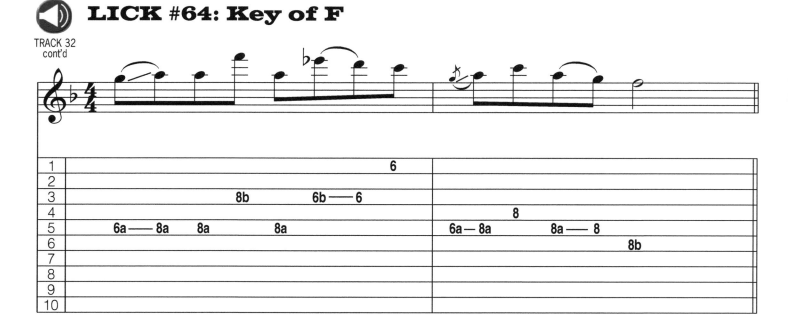

LICK #64: Key of F

1							6							
2														
3				8b		6b — 6								
4										8				
5	6a — 8a	8a		8a				6a — 8a		8a — 8				
6											8b			
7														
8														
9														
10														

LICK #65: Key of F

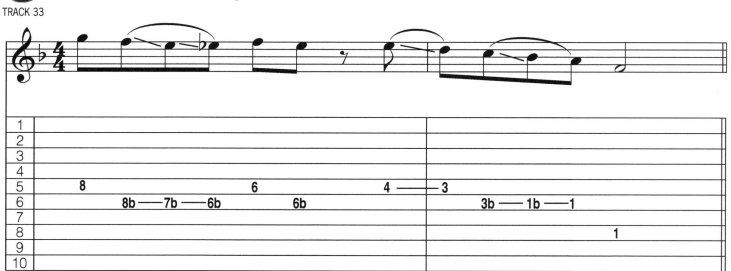

1								
2								
3								
4								
5	8			6		4 — 3		
6		8b — 7b — 6b		6b		3b — 1b — 1		
7								
8							1	
9								
10								

LICK #66: Key of B

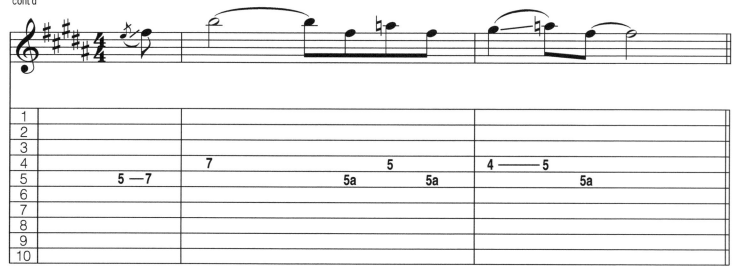

1					
2					
3					
4		7		5	4 — 5
5	5 — 7		5a	5a	5a
6					
7					
8					
9					
10					

LICK #67: Key of Bm

TRACK 34

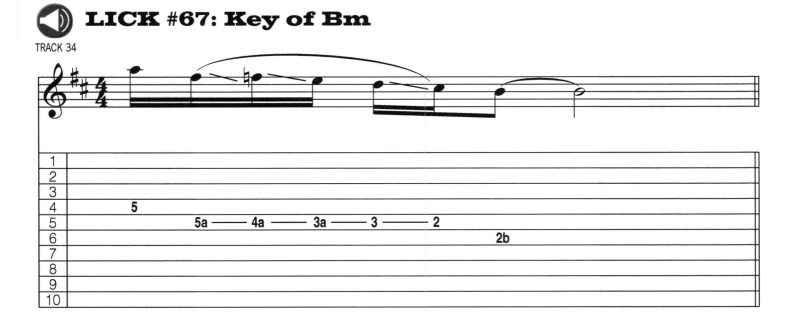

LICK #68: Key of Bm

TRACK 34
cont'd

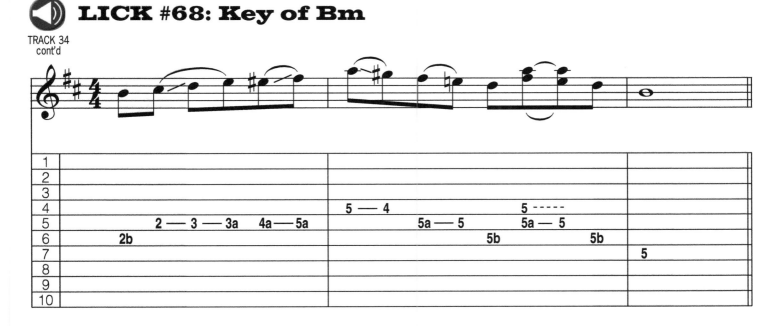

LICK #69: Key of B

TRACK 35

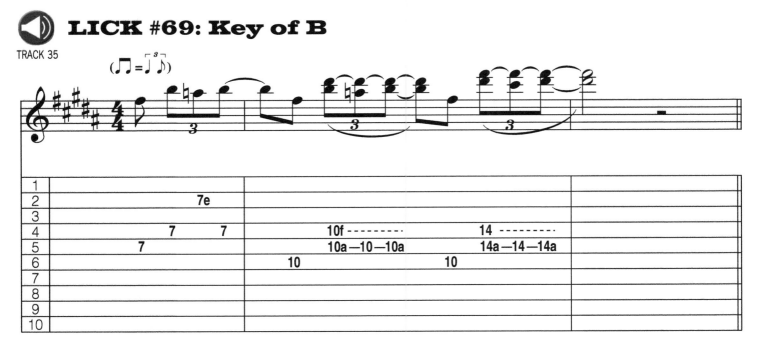

LICK #70: Key of B

TRACK 35
cont'd

8va throughout

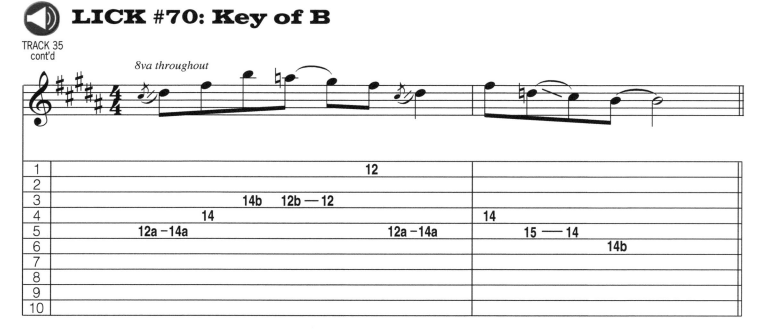

1	12	
2		
3	14b 12b — 12	
4	14	14
5	12a –14a 12a –14a	15 — 14
6		14b
7		
8		
9		
10		

LICK #71: Key of G

TRACK 36

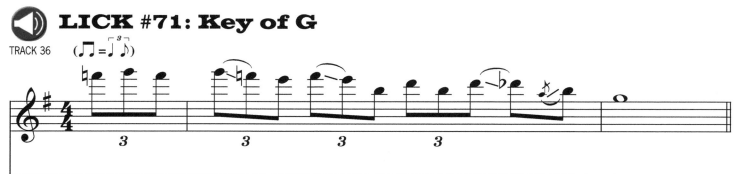

1		
2	15e 15e 13	
3		
4	15 15 — 13 13 —12 10 10 — 9	
5	10a 10a 8a—10a	
6		10b
7		
8		
9		
10		

LICK #72: Key of G

TRACK 36
cont'd

1		
2		8
3		
4		
5	10 8 — 8a	8a — 8
6	10b — 9b — 8b — 8	
7		
8		
9		
10		

LICK #73: Key of G

TRACK 37

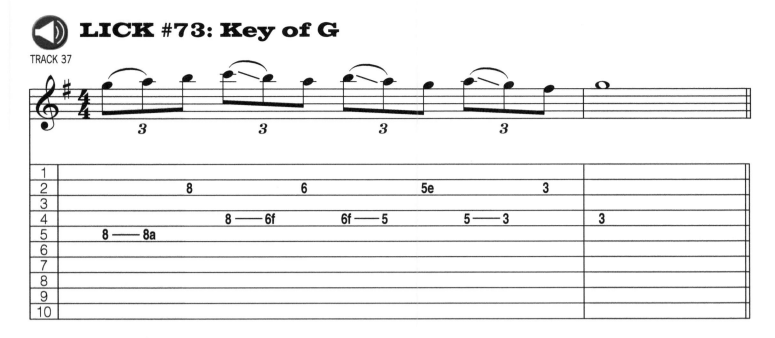

1												
2			8		6		5e		3			
3												
4			8 — 6f		6f — 5		5 — 3		3			
5	8 — 8a											
6												
7												
8												
9												
10												

LICK #74: Key of G

TRACK 37
cont'd

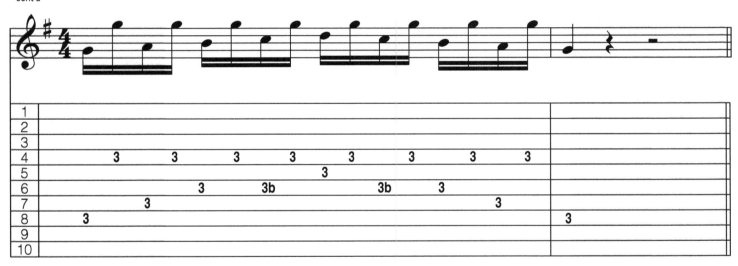

1										
2										
3										
4		3	3	3	3	3	3	3	3	
5						3				
6			3	3b		3b	3			
7		3						3		
8	3								3	
9										
10										

LICK #75: Key of G

TRACK 38

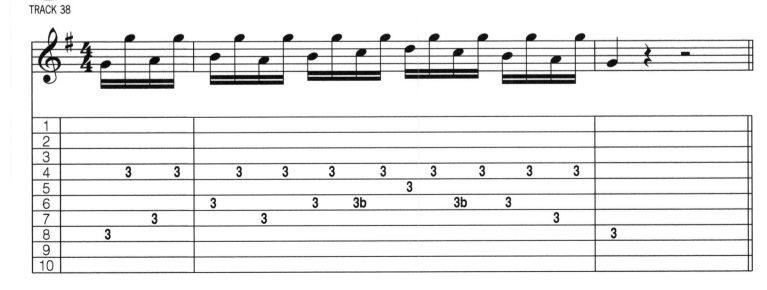

1											
2											
3											
4		3	3	3	3	3	3	3	3		
5							3				
6			3		3	3b		3b	3		
7		3		3					3		
8	3									3	
9											
10											

LICK #76: Key of D

TRACK 38
cont'd

LICK #77: Key of D

TRACK 39

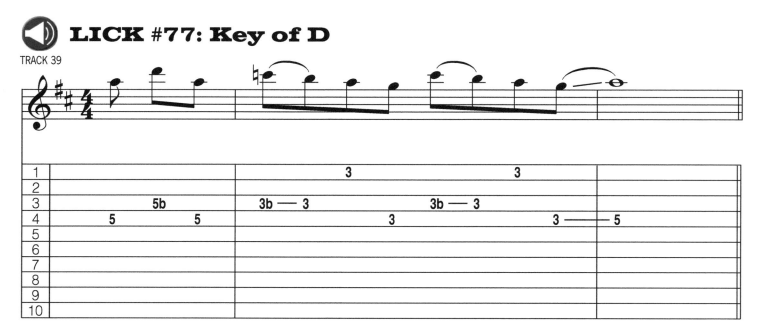

LICK #78: Key of D

TRACK 39
cont'd

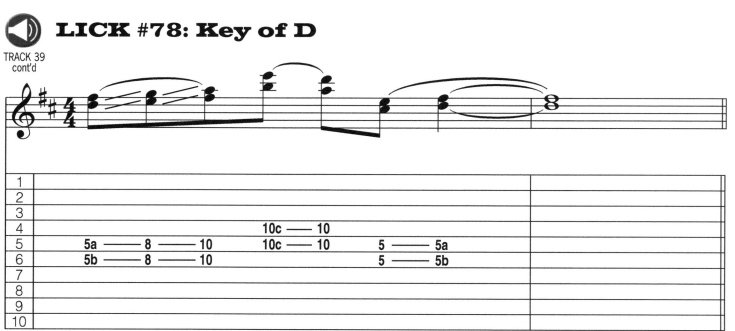

LICK #79: Key of D

TRACK 40

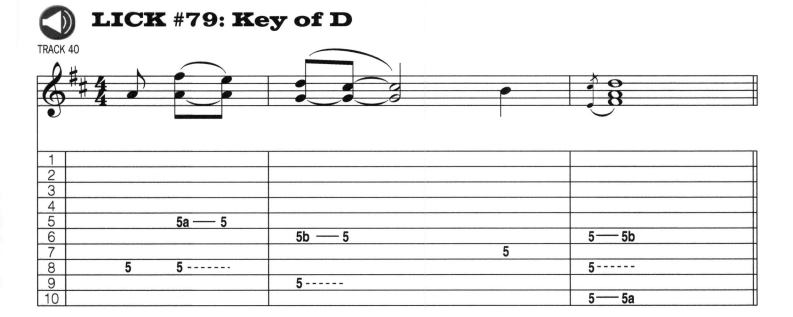

1					
2					
3					
4					
5		5a — 5			
6			5b — 5		5 — 5b
7				5	
8		5 5 -------			5 ------
9			5 ------		
10					5 —— 5a

LICK #80: Key of D

TRACK 40
cont'd

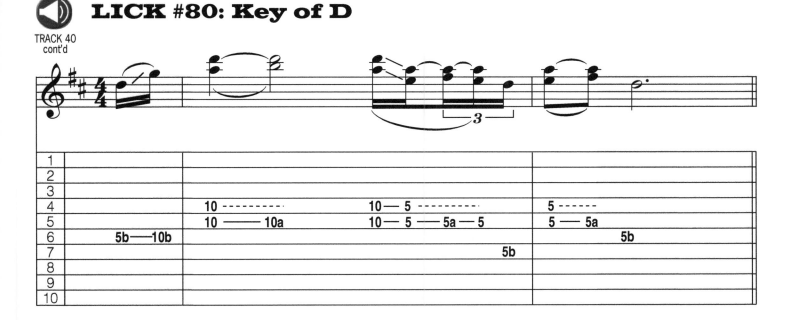

1					
2					
3					
4		10 ----------	10 — 5 ----------	5 ------	
5		10 —— 10a	10 — 5 — 5a — 5	5 — 5a	
6	5b——10b			5b	
7			5b		
8					
9					
10					

LICK #81: Key of Cm

TRACK 41

1			6			
2		6				
3						
4			6	6 — 5	6 —— 5	
5		6—6a	6a		6a — 6	
6					6b — 6	
7						6
8						
9						
10						

LICK #82: Key of Cm

TRACK 41
cont'd

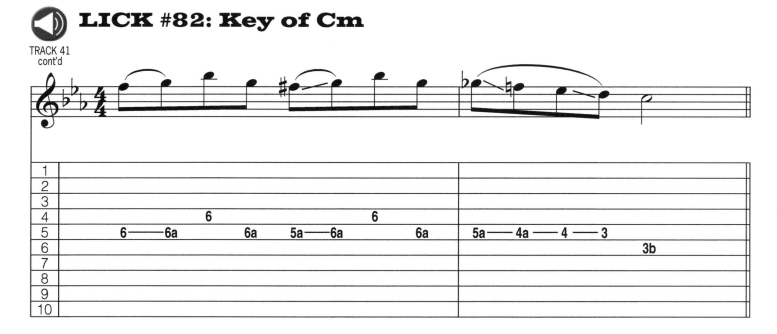

LICK #83: Key of C

TRACK 42

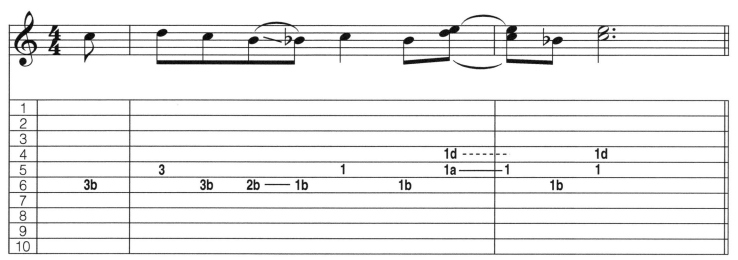

 ## LICK #84: Key of C

TRACK 42
cont'd

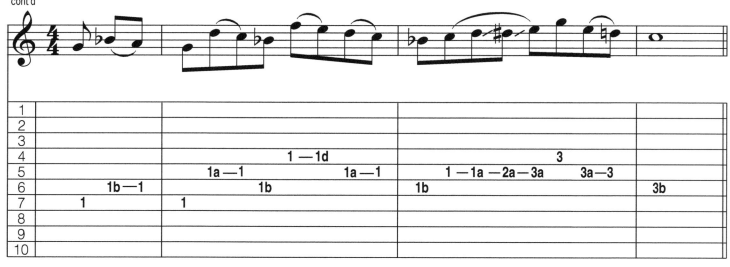

LICK #85: Key of C

TRACK 43

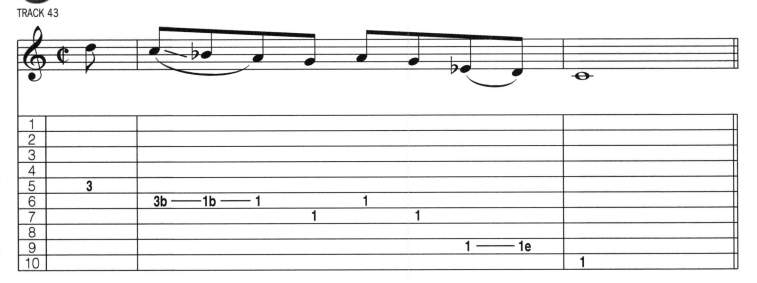

1				
2				
3				
4				
5	3			
6		3b ——1b —— 1	1	
7			1 1	
8				
9			1 —— 1e	
10				1

LICK #86: Key of A

TRACK 43
cont'd

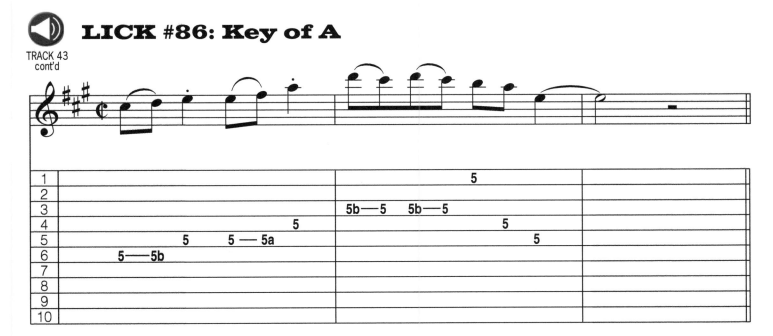

1		5	
2			
3		5b—5 5b—5	
4	5	5	
5	5 5 — 5a	5	
6	5——5b		
7			
8			
9			
10			

LICK #87: Key of A

TRACK 44

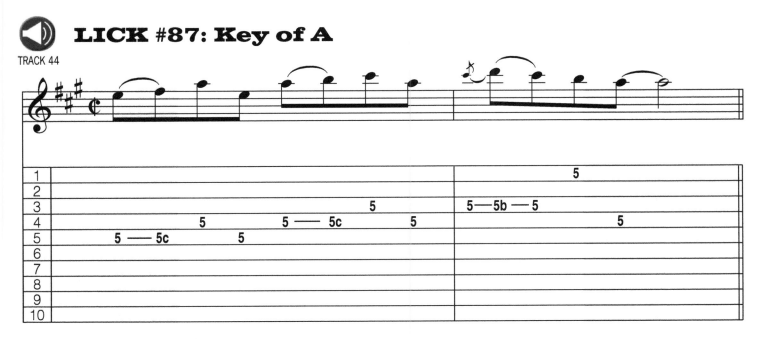

1		5
2		
3	5	5—5b — 5
4	5 5 — 5c 5	5
5	5 — 5c 5	
6		
7		
8		
9		
10		

LICK #88: Key of A

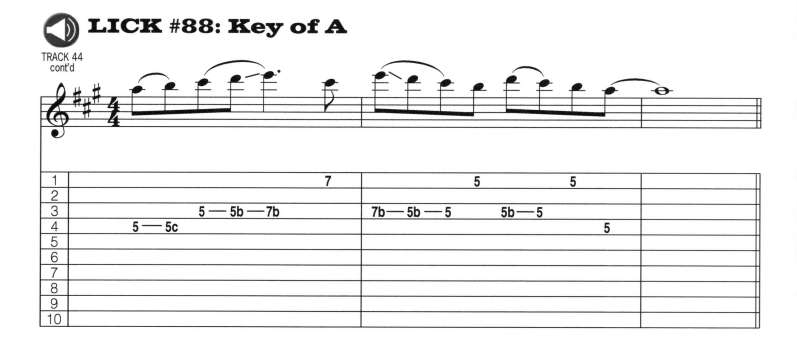

							7			5		5		
1							7			5		5		
2														
3					5 — 5b — 7b				7b — 5b — 5			5b — 5		
4			5 — 5c										5	
5														
6														
7														
8														
9														
10														

LICK #89: Key of A

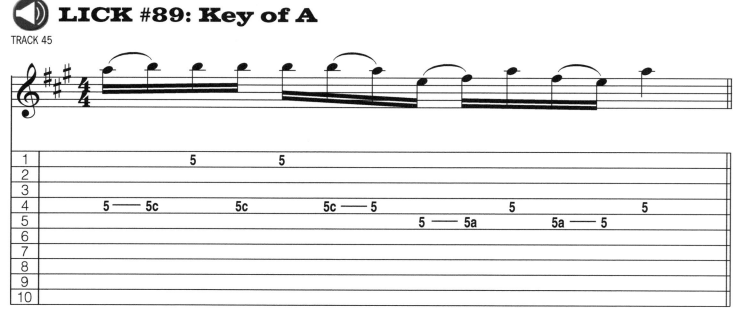

			5		5							
1			5		5							
2												
3												
4		5 — 5c		5c		5c — 5			5		5
5							5 — 5a		5a — 5		
6											
7											
8											
9											
10											

LICK #90: Key of A

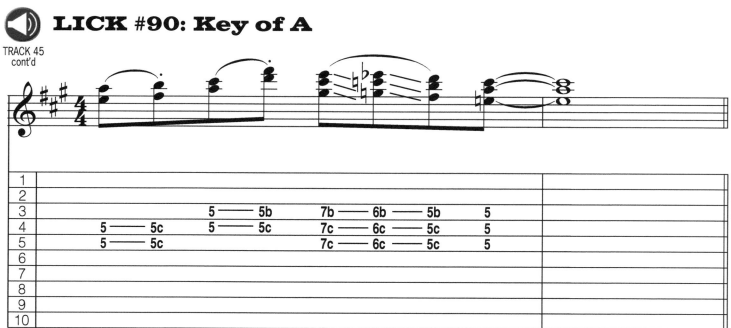

1									
2									
3				5 — 5b	7b — 6b — 5b	5			
4		5 — 5c	5 — 5c	7c — 6c — 5c	5			
5		5 — 5c		7c — 6c — 5c	5			
6									
7									
8									
9									
10									

LICK #91: Key of F

TRACK 46

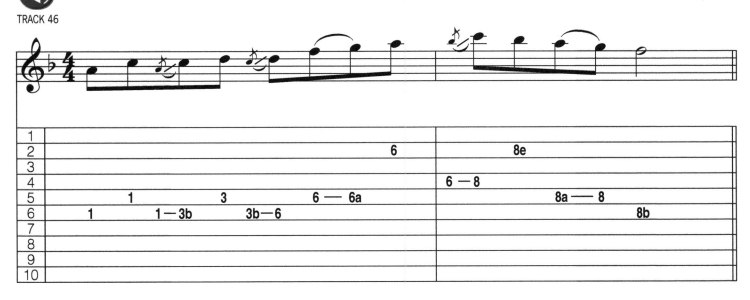

LICK #92: Key of F

TRACK 46
cont'd

LICK #93: Key of F

TRACK 47

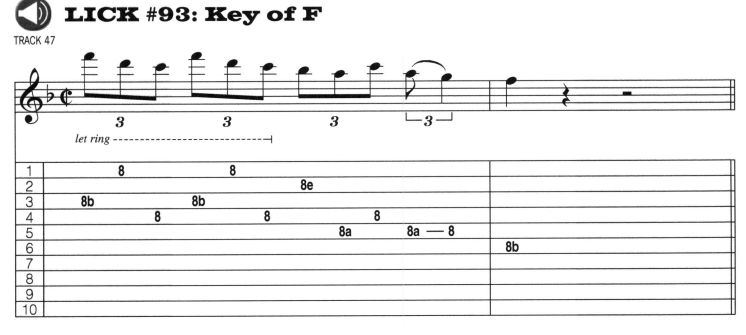

LICK #94: Key of F

1			8		8		6				
2								6			
3			8b — 8								
4			8			8	6		6 — 5 — 3		
5		8a								3a — 4a	
6											
7											
8											
9											
10											

LICK #95: Key of F

1								
2		4						
3								
4								
5		4a — 3a — 3		3				
6				3b	3b — 1b — 1	1b — 1		
7							1	
8							1d — 1	
9								
10								

LICK #96: Key of E

8va -

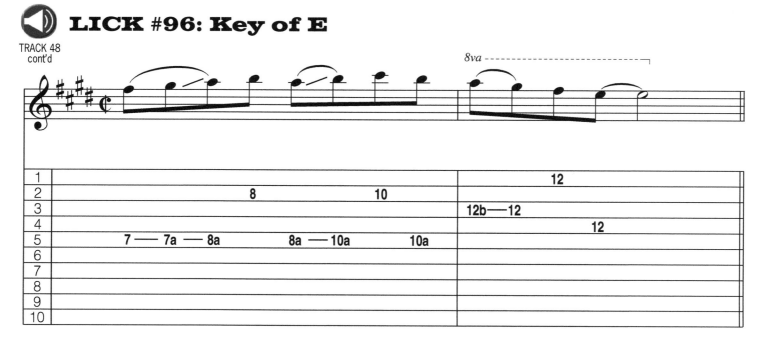

1								12	
2				8		10			
3							12b — 12		
4								12	
5		7 — 7a — 8a			8a — 10a	10a			
6									
7									
8									
9									
10									

LICK #97: Key of E

TRACK 49

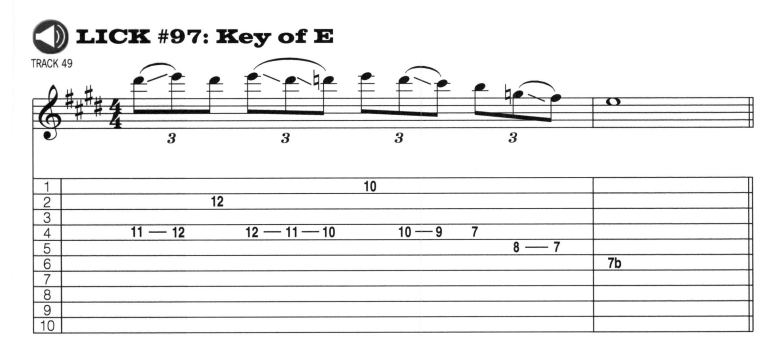

LICK #98: Key of Em

TRACK 49
cont'd

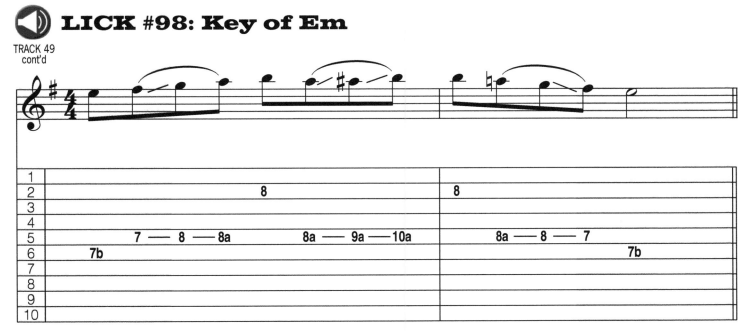

LICK #99: Key of E

TRACK 50

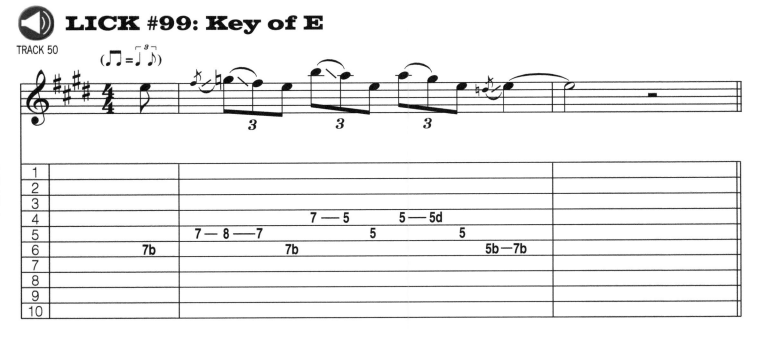

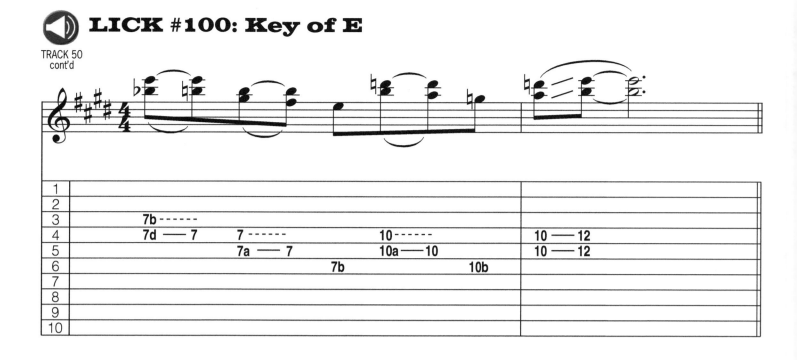

LICK #100: Key of E

TRACK 50
cont'd

TOP COUNTRY HITS

Arranged for piano and voice with guitar chords.

Top Country Hits of 2019-2020
18 of the best country songs from 2019 to 2020: All to Myself • Beer Never Broke My Heart • The Bones • Even Though I'm Leaving • Girl • God's Country • I Don't Know About You • Look What God Gave Her • Miss Me More • Old Town Road (Remix) • One Man Band • One Thing Right • Prayed for You • Rainbow • Remember You Young • 10,000 Hours • What If I Never Get over You • Whiskey Glasses.

00334223...$17.99

Top Country Hits of 2018-2019
18 Hot Singles

18 of the year's hottest country hits arranged for piano, voice and guitar. Includes: Best Shot (Jimmie Allen) • Drowns the Whiskey (Jason Aldean) • Get Along (Kenny Chesney) • Hangin' On (Chris Young) • Heaven (Kane Brown) • Love Wins (Carrie Underwood) • Mercy (Brett Young) • Rich (Maren Morris) • She Got the Best of Me (Luke Combs) • Simple (Florida Georgia Line) • Up Down (Morgan Wallen feat. Florida Georgia Line) • and more.

00289814...$17.99

Top Country Hits of 2017-2018
18 of the year's top toe-tapping, twangy hits: Body like a Back Road • Broken Halos • Craving You • Dear Hate • Dirt on My Boots • Dirty Laundry • Drinkin' Problem • Fighter • Hurricane • Legends • Meant to Be • Millionaire • Yours • and more.

00267160...$17.99

Top Country Hits of 2015-2016
14 of the year's most popular country songs: Burning House (Cam) • Biscuits (Kacey Musgraves) • Girl Crush (Little Big Town) • I'm Comin' Over (Chris Young) • Let Me See You Girl (Cole Swindell) • Smoke Break (Carrie Underwood) • Strip It Down (Luke Bryan) • Take Your Time (Sam Hunt) • Traveller (Chris Stapleton) • and more.

00156297...$16.99

Top Country Hits of 2014-2015
14 of the year's most popular country songs. Includes: American Kids (Kenny Chesney) • Day Drinking (Little Big Town) • I See You (Luke Bryan) • Neon Light (Blake Shelton) • Payback (Rascal Flatts) • Shotgun Rider (Tim McGraw) • Something in the Water (Carrie Underwood) • Sunshine & Whiskey (Frankie Ballard) • Talladega (Eric Church) • and more.

00142574...$16.99

Top Country Hits of 2013-2014
15 of today's most recognizable hits from country's hottest stars, including: Carolina (Parmalee) • Cruise (Florida Georgia Line) • Drunk Last Night (Eli Young Band) • Mine Would Be You (Blake Shelton) • Southern Girl (Tim McGraw) • That's My Kind of Night (Luke Bryan) • We Were Us (Keith Urban and Miranda Lambert) • and more.

00125359...$16.99

Top Country Hits of 2012-2013
Features 15 fantastic country hits: Beer Money • Begin Again • Better Dig Two • Come Wake Me Up • Every Storm (Runs Out of Rain) • Fastest Girl in Town • Hard to Love • Kiss Tomorrow Goodbye • The One That Got Away • Over You • Red • Take a Little Ride • Til My Last Day • Wanted • We Are Never Ever Getting Back Together.

00118291...$14.99

HAL•LEONARD®

Prices, content and availability subject to change without notice.

THE ULTIMATE COLLECTION OF
FAKE BOOKS

The Real Book – Sixth Edition

Hal Leonard proudly presents the first legitimate and legal editions of these books ever produced. These bestselling titles are mandatory for anyone who plays jazz! Over 400 songs, including: All By Myself • Dream a Little Dream of Me • God Bless the Child • Like Someone in Love • When I Fall in Love • and more.

00240221 Volume 1, C Instruments.................$45.00
00240224 Volume 1, Bb Instruments................$45.00
00240225 Volume 1, Eb Instruments................$45.00
00240226 Volume 1, BC Instruments...............$45.00

**Go to halleonard.com
to view all *Real Books* available**

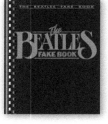

The Beatles Fake Book

200 of the Beatles' hits: All You Need Is Love • Blackbird • Can't Buy Me Love • Day Tripper • Eleanor Rigby • The Fool on the Hill • Hey Jude • In My Life • Let It Be • Michelle • Norwegian Wood (This Bird Has Flown) • Penny Lane • Revolution • She Loves You • Twist and Shout • With a Little Help from My Friends • Yesterday • and many more!
00240069 C Instruments...........$39.99

The Best Fake Book Ever

More than 1,000 songs from all styles of music: All My Loving • At the Hop • Cabaret • Dust in the Wind • Fever • Hello, Dolly • Hey Jude • King of the Road • Longer • Misty • Route 66 • Sentimental Journey • Somebody • Song Sung Blue • Spinning Wheel • Unchained Melody • We Will Rock You • What a Wonderful World • Wooly Bully • Y.M.C.A. • and more.

00290239 C Instruments....................$49.99
00240084 Eb Instruments..................$49.95

The Celtic Fake Book

Over 400 songs from Ireland, Scotland and Wales: Auld Lang Syne • Barbara Allen • Danny Boy • Finnegan's Wake • The Galway Piper • Irish Rover • Loch Lomond • Molly Malone • My Bonnie Lies Over the Ocean • My Wild Irish Rose • That's an Irish Lullaby • and more. Includes Gaelic lyrics where applicable and a pronunciation guide.
00240153 C Instruments...........$25.00

Classic Rock Fake Book

Over 250 of the best rock songs of all time: American Woman • Beast of Burden • Carry On Wayward Son • Dream On • Free Ride • Hurts So Good • I Shot the Sheriff • Layla • My Generation • Nights in White Satin • Owner of a Lonely Heart • Rhiannon • Roxanne • Summer of '69 • We Will Rock You • You Ain't Seen Nothin' Yet • and lots more!
00240108 C Instruments....................$35.00

Classical Fake Book

This unprecedented, amazingly comprehensive reference includes over 850 classical themes and melodies for all classical music lovers. Includes everything from Renaissance music to Vivaldi and Mozart to Mendelssohn. Lyrics in the original language are included when appropriate.
00240044 ....$39.99

The Disney Fake Book

Even more Disney favorites, including: The Bare Necessities • Can You Feel the Love Tonight • Circle of Life • How Do You Know? • Let It Go • Part of Your World • Reflection • Some Day My Prince Will Come • When I See an Elephant Fly • You'll Be in My Heart • and many more.
00175311 C Instruments...........$34.99
Disney characters & artwork TM & © 2021 Disney

The Folksong Fake Book

Over 1,000 folksongs: Bury Me Not on the Lone Prairie • Clementine • The Erie Canal • Go, Tell It on the Mountain • Home on the Range • Kumbaya • Michael Row the Boat Ashore • Shenandoah • Simple Gifts • Swing Low, Sweet Chariot • When Johnny Comes Marching Home • Yankee Doodle • and many more.
00240151 ....$34.99

The Hal Leonard Real Jazz Standards Fake Book

Over 250 standards in easy-to-read authentic hand-written jazz engravings: Ain't Misbehavin' • Blue Skies • Crazy He Calls Me • Desafinado (Off Key) • Fever • How High the Moon • It Don't Mean a Thing (If It Ain't Got That Swing) • Lazy River • Mood Indigo • Old Devil Moon • Route 66 • Satin Doll • Witchcraft • and more.
00240161 C Instruments..............................$45.00

The Hymn Fake Book

Nearly 1,000 multi-denominational hymns perfect for church musicians or hobbyists: Amazing Grace • Christ the Lord Is Risen Today • For the Beauty of the Earth • It Is Well with My Soul • A Mighty Fortress Is Our God • O for a Thousand Tongues to Sing • Praise to the Lord, the Almighty • Take My Life and Let It Be • What a Friend We Have in Jesus • and hundreds more!
00240145 C Instruments...........................$29.99

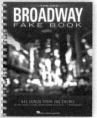

The New Broadway Fake Book

This amazing collection includes 645 songs from 285 shows: All I Ask of You • Any Dream Will Do • Close Every Door • Consider Yourself • Dancing Queen • Mack the Knife • Mamma Mia • Memory • The Phantom of the Opera • Popular • Strike up the Band • and more!
00138905 C Instruments............$45.00

The Praise & Worship Fake Book

Over 400 songs including: Amazing Grace (My Chains Are Gone) • Cornerstone • Everlasting God • Great Are You Lord • In Christ Alone • Mighty to Save • Open the Eyes of My Heart • Shine, Jesus, Shine • This Is Amazing Grace • and more.
00160838 C Instruments...........$39.99
00240324 Bb Instruments.........$34.99

Three Chord Songs Fake Book

200 classic and contemporary 3-chord tunes in melody/lyric/chord format: Ain't No Sunshine • Bang a Gong (Get It On) • Cold, Cold Heart • Don't Worry, Be Happy • Give Me One Reason • I Got You (I Feel Good) • Kiss • Me and Bobby McGee • Rock This Town • Werewolves of London • You Don't Mess Around with Jim • and more.
00240387 ....$34.99

The Ultimate Christmas Fake Book

The 6th edition of this bestseller features over 270 traditional and contemporary Christmas hits: Have Yourself a Merry Little Christmas • I'll Be Home for Christmas O Come, All Ye Faithful (Adeste Fideles) • Santa Baby • Winter Wonderland • and more.
00147215 C Instruments...........$30.00

The Ultimate Country Fake Book

This book includes over 700 of your favorite country hits: Always on My Mind • Boot Scootin' Boogie • Crazy • Down at the Twist and Shout • Forever and Ever, Amen • Friends in Low Places • The Gambler • Jambalaya • King of the Road • Sixteen Tons • There's a Tear in My Beer • Your Cheatin' Heart • and hundreds more.
00240049 C Instruments.....................$49.99

The Ultimate Fake Book

Includes over 1,200 hits: Blue Skies • Body and Soul • Endless Love • Isn't It Romantic? • Memory • Mona Lisa • Moon River • Operator • Piano Man • Roxanne • Satin Doll • Shout • Small World • Smile • Speak Softly, Love • Strawberry Fields Forever • Tears in Heaven • Unforgettable • hundreds more!
00240024 C Instruments...........$55.00
00240026 Bb Instruments.................$49.95

The Ultimate Jazz Fake Book

This must-own collection includes 635 songs spanning all jazz styles from more than 9 decades. Songs include: Maple Leaf Rag • Basin Street Blues • A Night in Tunisia • Lullaby of Birdland • The Girl from Ipanema • Bag's Groove • I Can't Get Started • All the Things You Are • and many more!
00240079 C Instruments...............$45.00
00240080 Bb Instruments................$45.00
00240081 Eb Instruments.................$45.00

The Ultimate Rock Pop Fake Book

This amazing collection features nearly 550 rock and pop hits: American Pie • Bohemian Rhapsody • Born to Be Wild • Clocks • Dancing with Myself • Eye of the Tiger • Proud Mary • Rocket Man • Should I Stay or Should I Go • Total Eclipse of the Heart • Unchained Melody • When Doves Cry • Y.M.C.A. • You Raise Me Up • and more.
00240310 C Instruments...............$39.99

**Complete songlists available online at
www.halleonard.com**

HAL•LEONARD®